THE BEGINNER WITCH'S GUIDE TO GRIMIORES

Everything You Need To Know About Creating, Acquiring, and Using Your Own Magical Spell Book

JULIE WILDER

CONTENTS

Also by Julie Wilder — v
Don't Forget Your Free Book! — vii

1. My Magical Philosophy — 1
2. Grimoire Basics — 11
3. How A Grimoire Can Strengthen Your Magical Power — 13

Types of Grimoires — 19

4. What To Put In Your Grimoire — 51
5. How To Write Your Own Grimoire Spells — 59
6. Caring For Your Grimoire — 65
7. When To Release A Well-Loved Grimoire — 71
8. Final Thoughts — 77

Also by Julie Wilder — 81

Also by Julie Wilder

What Type of Witch Are You?
How to Become A Witch
Why Didn't My Spell Work?
Beginner Witch's Guide to Grimoires
Tarot for Beginner Witches

Don't Forget Your Free Book!

If you want to learn more ways to practice simple, secular witchcraft, be sure to pick up a **copy of this free book of spells**, and my **free Beginner Witch Starter kit** with printables, correspondences, meditations, and magical journaling prompts. Use the link below to get both of those!

https://whitewitchacademy.com/freebies

My Magical Philosophy

Hi! I'm Julie Wilder, writer, wanderer, personal development junkie, and a practicing witch. My goal in everything I write is to empower others to connect with their power and magic. In this book, I won't tell you how to practice your witchcraft and how to put together the perfect grimoire because I believe magic is highly personal. This is your magical practice, and I'll probably repeat that about seventy times throughout this book.

You might not agree with everything in this book, and that's totally fine. I believe it's important to really chew on things before you accept them. I believe that blazing your own trail is what witchcraft is all about.

I wrote this book for beginner witches who want to practice magic with a grimoire. This book will explain absolutely everything you need to know when you're ready to get your hands on your first (or fiftieth) grimoire. The Beginner's Guide to Grimoires is a concise, easy-to-follow guide written for modern witches who are ready to connect with their inner power and perform secular magic.

Here's exactly what we'll cover:

-What a grimoire is and how it can help your witchcraft

-How a grimoire differs from a Book of Shadows

-Different types of grimoires and their specific benefits

-How to pick the right grimoire for your lifestyle and magical needs

-What to write in a grimoire

-How to care for and cultivate a deep connection with your grimoire

This is the fourth book in my White Witch Academy Textbook Series. To get the other books, got to www.whitewitchacademy.com/books.

Secular Witchcraft

I write about and practice secular magic. It's the kind of witchcraft that can be paired with any religion or belief system. It doesn't matter if you're an atheist, a Buddhist, a Christian, a Muslim, or any other religion.

For a long time, I thought you had to be a Wiccan to be a witch. Not true! Wicca is a religion with its own set of rules, gods and goddesses, and traditions. Wiccans often consider themselves witches, but not all witches identify as Wiccans.

You might hear the term "Pagan" thrown around when you're talking about magic. Paganism is an umbrella term used for many different nature-based religions. Note the word *religion*. Paganism is a religion, just like Wicca, or Christianity, Hinduism, Islamism—you get the idea. Some Pagans also consider themselves witches, but not all witches identify as Pagans.

Make sense?

Secular witchcraft is magic that isn't based in any religion. Secular witches work with energy and the spiritual realm to create change in the physical world. Their practice is not guided by a set of rules, books, or specific gods or goddesses.

Maybe you've heard the Wiccan Rede which states that any magic you do to others will come back on you "threefold".

In secular witchcraft, you create your own system of ethics and moral guidelines. I choose not to curse people because I've found it to be a waste of my valuable energy. It doesn't make me feel better when someone suffers—even someone I don't like.

You might disagree, and there is room for that in secular witchcraft! I'm not going to tell you what to do. You make the rules, and you take responsibility for your actions.

So let go of any preconceived beliefs you have about witchcraft! Open your mind to the possibilities and let your intuition guide you. You can tap into the ancient, powerful magic of the universe *your way*.

How to Trust Your Intuition

I use the word "intuition" A LOT in everything I write and create. My witchcraft is led by my intuition. I recently learned that not everyone has a deep connection to their intuition.

If this is you, and you find your eyes glazing over every time people say things like, "Let your intuition guide you" and "Trust your intuition", don't sweat it! Let me explain what I mean when I talk about intuition.

For me, "intuition" refers to that wise, comforting, sometimes tough-love voice you hear whenever you face a new issue, conflict, thought, or belief. Some people refer to their intuition as an "instinct" or a "hunch". Sometimes your intuition will warn you when you're in danger. Other times, your intuition will push you to take a risk.

Have you ever walked into a room and thought something like, "This place feels homey" or "This cafe feels sad and depressing"? That's probably your intuition talking.

When you're introducing a new grimoire into your magical practice, you'll need to make many intuitive choices. You'll have to decide what kind of grimoire to use, where to get it, and what to write in it. To do this, you can ask other witches for advice. You can read books about grimoires, like this one. You can research the topic on the internet. But in the end, all that matters are the choices you make regarding your grimoire and your witchcraft.

I encourage myself to always trust my intuition above the opinions and recommendations of others. No one knows me, like me!

The tricky thing about intuition is that it isn't the only voice echoing around the labyrinth of your mind. You might also hear the voices of fear, past trauma, or social conditioning.

Note: most witches won't actually hear a voice. I'm referring to the thoughts, feelings, and images that zip through your mind.

For example, let's say you go on a date with a kind, interesting, attractive person. You have a lot of fun laughing and sharing stories with each other. You feel a real connection to this person. Then you leave your date knowing that you want to see this person again. That "knowing" could be your intuition nudging you toward your desires—a healthy, joyful relationship.

Then you get home and you second guess yourself. You have thoughts like, "This person is too good to be true", "I should end this thing before I get hurt", or "I don't have time for a relationship right now". Personally, I would classify these thoughts as fear-based, and I don't think they are likely coming from your intuition.

Here's The Major Difference:

Your intuition will always be the voice that feels bold, expansive and full of possibility.

Your fear-based voice is the opposite. It will urge you toward choices that seem safe, small, familiar, and contracting.

What If You Still Aren't Sure?

Sometimes I feel like I'm being pulled into two different directions, and both directions feel equally wonderful. When this happens, it's hard to understand what your intuition is telling you.

In my experience, the solution is to *just pick one*. Make a choice and don't overthink it. Then take notice of your thoughts and feelings following your decision. Do you feel excited, hopeful, and buoyant? Do you regret your choice immediately after you make it? If so, why? Are you scared of the growth that might come from your new path, or are you sad because you realized you only picked this course of action based on other people's perception of you?

Pay attention to everything you think and feel as you lean further into your choice. If you do this often enough, you'll start to notice patterns. You'll learn to recognize what it feels like when you're being guided by your intuition.

That's how I define intuition in a nutshell. It's not as mystical or woo-woo as some people make it out to be. It's just about listening to yourself!

Whatever you do, don't beat yourself up for ignoring your intuition. Even the most magical, enlightened witch will not maintain "perfect alignment" to themselves and the universe at all times. Noticing those intuitive nudges takes practice, and lots of trial and error. Be gentle and loving to yourself.

I believe I have a decent connection to my intuition, but I know that sometimes I still make choices out of fear. So what? Making mistakes is what being human is all about. Embrace it. Each decision (right or wrong) reveals a lesson that will deepen your magical practice.

Yes, you are magical.

Yes, you are powerful.

Yes, you have everything inside of you need to have a beautiful, wonderful, creative, adventurous, magical life.

Seriously.

My Witchcraft Journey

Are you shaking your head, being all, "Maybe that's possible for you, Julie, but not for me,"?

If so, that's OK. I *so* get it. I used to think I was broken, defective and incapable of taking care of myself. I used to let fear hold me back. I thought money, fun jobs, and a fulfilling romantic relationship were things that other (better) people could have—not me.

Witchcraft helped me understand and trust in my inner strength and my intuition.

I started casting spells, taking risks, and accepting the gifts that came floating down from the universe.

I want you to know that you might never feel you're "ready" to cast powerful spells and make your life awesome. You might always have that I'm-not-doing-this-right feeling. You'll probably always feel a little scared when you're stepping out of your comfort zone.

Do it anyway.

I've seen in my own life—and in the lives of my friends—that "readiness" has nothing to do with your success. It all comes down to if you DO THE THING or not.

I'm currently living a life that I deeply enjoy. I got here by doing things that felt a little too big and bold for someone like me. I wrote a book, then another. Now I have eleven books across two pen names, and I'm so proud to tell people what I do.

Witchcraft made me believe I was powerful, and that belief unlocked the door to a life of joyful creativity and delicious challenge.

I'm a witch, and so are you—if you want to be. I'm no different than you. I'm not more powerful or enlightened. I'm just a woman who got her tarot cards read one day and decided to explore the metaphysical aspects of this world.

I believe everyone is born with inherent magical power, and because of that, I believe everyone can be a witch. For me, witchcraft is a choice. I don't believe that you need to be from a magical family or that you have to be "psychic"—or any of those other witchy myths that some people use to keep others from exploring the wonders of magic.

So what do you think? Does this sound right to you?

Take a moment to listen to the whispers of your intuition.

If you hear a resounding "yes", read on, my witchy friend!

Grimoire Basics

What is a Grimoire?

A grimoire is a magical book that witches use in their witchcraft. It's a spell book—plain and simple! This special magical tool is one of the most personal aspects of a witch's practice. Each grimoire is as unique as the witch themselves, and every witch deserves to have a grimoire that perfectly suits their individual lifestyle. It's not a one-size-fits-all kind of thing!

We all have different talents, preferences, and upbringings. A witch might find they are intuitively drawn to certain types of grimoires over others. A witch might use more than one throughout their lifetime—sometimes one for each type of magic they perform.

As you read through this book, I invite you to

take notes on which grimoires you're most curious about. Afterwards, you can experiment with the different types of grimoires and see for yourself which serve your spiritual practice the best.

Your grimoire doesn't have to be some old dusty spell book with tattered yellowing pages. It could be a shoebox of notecards, a video blog, or a done-for-you published spell book. There are a wide range of grimoires available to you, and we'll take a deep dive into each one!

What's the Difference Between a Grimoire and a Book Of Shadows?

There's one and only one fundamental difference between a grimoire and a Book of Shadows.

A **Book of Shadows** is a type of grimoire that is specifically used by a witch who follows the Wiccan path. You'll see if capitalized most of the time. It's a term used only in Wicca, and you'll almost always see it capitalized.

A **grimoire** is the general term for a spell book used across almost every witchcraft practice. As a secular witch, I call my magical book a grimoire. My friend, who is a Wiccan, has her Book of Shadows.

Despite the difference in name, a grimoire and a Book of Shadows share the same purpose—**to document and guide a witch on their magical practice.**

How A Grimoire Can Strengthen Your Magical Power

Using a grimoire in your magical practice is a great way for a witch to deepen their connection to witchcraft. **Here are some reasons a grimoire can benefit a witch:**

Grimoires give you a way to remember specific incantations and the steps of your spells.

A grimoire provides a place for you to record all your spells step-by-step, in as much detail as you want. You can use your grimoire to draw pictures of your altar setups, add notes in the margins where you made changes to a spell, and polish your incantations and intentions. Then you can go back again to perform these personalized spells.

You can look back and see what your favorite forms of magic are.

As you use your grimoire, you'll notice what your favorite spells are. You might discover that you love any spell that uses moon energy, or that you have the most success when you're performing fire magic. These are all clues that can help you pinpoint your natural magical strengths, preferences and inclinations.

From these observations, you might decide to focus more time and energy on a certain type of magic—such as lunar magic. Then you can be on the lookout for more tools that relate to the moon like selenite crystals, moon-charged elixirs, and items that are white, blue or purple.

You can discover your creative style by decorating with your grimoire.

Get in touch with your personal magical aesthetic as you bond with grimoire! Keep meaningful items pressed between the pages like dried herbs, ribbons, photographs, and handwritten letters from friends. Cover the outside of the book with colored fabric, wrapping paper, or a knitted book sleeve. Draw symbols on the spine. Make a collage with an old deck of tarot cards. Jot down notes with different colored pens.

Notice what colors, patterns, and symbols you use most. Try to incorporate these into your altars and witchcraft as much as possible, and see if that brings more joy and power to your magic. The more you understand your own preferences and natural leanings, the more powerful you'll become.

You can track the results of your spells.

A grimoire can provide a place for you to note results of your spells. Consider including things like whether your spell manifested, how long it took, and the details of the manifestation. It may also be helpful to write down your mood in the days following your spell and any feelings that came up once you saw the results of your spell.

If your spell didn't work, experiment with small tweaks like a scientist testing a theory. Try different cleansing methods or different magic tools, and see what happens. Note the time, date, your current energy, the moon phase, the place you performed the spells, and any other relevant information you can think of.

Soon, you might notice patterns. For example, you might discover that you get your most accurate tarot card readings on Friday nights after a fun family dinner, or under the light of the full moon. Maybe you notice that your love spells are highly effective, but your money spells take longer to manifest. Record all of that in your grimoire, and do so without judgement. All of that is simply information to add depth to your witchcraft practice.

You can see how you've grown on your spiritual journey.

Do you ever go back and read your old diary entries, old book reports, or watch old videos of yourself and marvel at how much you've grown and matured? You can do the same thing with your grimoire. Over time, you'll see how your spells change and develop. You'll get more comfortable with your power and branch out into less familiar areas of witchcraft. Notice how your intentions become sharper and more potent. Appreciate the ebb and flow of your magic over the days, months, and years.

You can feel connected to other witches.

Grimoires are part of the witchcraft tradition. When you write in your grimoire, you are following in the footsteps of many other powerful witches who came before you. There is power in following tradition. When you are performing spells written by the witches who came before you, you are honoring the work they did and continuing their legacy. Even if you are making your grimoire from scratch, you are still tapping into this sacred tradition because the very act of writing in a grimoire is something that witches have been doing for ages. Plus, the grimoire that you create today might someday get into the hands of a new witch in future generations.

TYPES OF GRIMOIRES

Published Grimoires

If you're looking for a simple way to jumpstart your magical journey, you may enjoy working with a published grimoire.

Many bookstores, big box stores, and online shops sell a variety of quality grimoires at all different price points.

I've seen some ebook grimoires priced under five dollars. You can also get my starter grimoire for free at www.whitewitchacademy.com/freebies.

Some of the larger dictionary-sized hardcovers are more expensive, ranging from twenty to forty dollars and beyond. My favorite published grimoire is one by Judith Illes. You can get that at www.whitwhitchacademy.com/resources.

I enjoy using published grimoires because they are packed with lots of spells for you to experiment with. You don't have to wait for a family member to pass down their spell book. You don't have to scour the internet for quality spells. Just open your grimoire and start spellcasting!

Often, the book will include interesting information about the history of witchcraft and detailed instructions for how to use a variety of magical tools. I've seen some that include all kinds of helpful correspondences such as color meanings, numerology and herbal energies.

The downside of using a published grimoire is that these books tend to be large and heavy. They aren't easy to slip into a purse or hide away in your pocket for on-the-fly spells.

Another drawback is that these grimoires contain too much information. You might not need to know all those spells at this point in your magical journey. Maybe you won't need to know them ever! Trust me, it is not fun to dig through pages and pages of irrelevant spells before you find the one you need. This process can be overwhelming—even for the most seasoned witches.

Keep in mind that these books can be more expensive than a basic notebook. Don't let money impede your magical practice! If a published grimoire is out of your budget, check out your local library to see if they have any witchcraft books or grimoires available to borrow. This allows you to try out different grimoires before committing to one.

Tips For Using A Published Grimoire:

-Make sure you do your own research when working with historical spells. Some historical spells use ingredients that aren't safe to handle or ingest. Most published grimoires will include warnings and disclaimers with these kinds of spells, but it's always best to do some additional research to make sure you're not putting yourself or your loved ones at risk.

-If you don't want other people knowing about your magic, consider covering the outside of your book with paper or use the book jacket of another book to disguise it.

-Place sticky notes on the pages or scribble symbols in the margins to mark your favorite spells or document your results.

-Spend some time "bonding" with your grimoire before you use it to perform any spells. Cleanse it with your favorite cleansing spell to get rid of any lingering energy from the bookstore or warehouse it came from.

-Don't limit yourself to the spells and correspondences that are listed in the grimoire. Allow yourself to create your own spellcasting methods and magical meanings. Just because the book says the color red is associated with love spells doesn't mean you can't try to cast a love spell with a blue candle. Likewise, just because a spell calls for a sage bundle doesn't mean you can't substitute it for something else that you have on hand! The info in a grimoire should inspire you to tap into your own power and inner knowing!

Hand-Me-Down Grimoires

A hand-me-down grimoire is any magical spell book that was previously owned and used by another witch. A loved one may give you a grimoire, or you might find one hidden away in an attic somewhere. Another way to acquire a hand-me-down grimoire is to purchase one at a used bookstore, thrift shop, garage sale or library sale.

You might also get one through the mysterious forces of the universe. I received my first grimoire even before I began my path as a witch. I was sitting outside at a coffee shop one day when some man walked up to me and handed me a journal with a pentagram drawn on it. Inside were pages of handwritten spells, witchy sketches, and magical notes.

To be honest, it wasn't my type of grimoire. It was a black notebook with red drawings on the front—not my aesthetic at all. I love bright, cheerful pastel watercolors.

Yes, I know. The saying goes, "Don't judge a book by its cover". I disagree. I believe it's helpful to feel connected to *every aspect* of your new grimoire—visually, energetically, and intellectually. Go ahead, judge the heck out of your new grimoire's cover! That's your prerogative as a witch!

When I paged through this grimoire, I felt even more repelled. I found the handwriting on this particular grimoire hard to read, and a lot of the drawings were confusing.

I knew little about energy and magic. At that point, I didn't even know modern witchcraft was a thing—but this gifted grimoire made me feel uncomfortable.

This grimoire and I weren't a good fit. Did that mean the grimoire was bad? No. Did that mean I wasn't in touch with my magic? No.

It meant that this grimoire wasn't meant to be kept or used by me. I do not know why this man handed me this grimoire, and I don't think it matters much! It was his grimoire to give away, and it was up to me to decide what to do with it. I promptly threw it out in the nearest public trash can.

The lesson here is that if you receive a grimoire that doesn't "feel good" when you hold it or page through it, don't second guess yourself. Don't worry about hurting someone's feelings. Just don't use it!

You have options. Consider storing it somewhere until you feel ready to use it, giving it back to the person it belonged to, passing it along to a friend, or donating it. Maybe the best course of action is to throw the darn thing out. *You* get to decide. This is your witchcraft practice, and there is no reason to feel guilty, shameful or inadequate if you sense a mismatch of energy between you and a particular spell book.

That being said, a hand-me-down grimoire can feel incredibly special and powerful if it matches your energy. If one of these magical books comes your way, stay open and allow your intuition to help you decide if and how to use this grimoire!

Tips For Using A Hand-Me-Down Grimoire

-It's especially important to be aware of the energy of a hand-me-down grimoire. The energy attached to an object directly affects the results of whatever magic it's used in. For example, if you don't feel connected to the book's current energy (like in my situation with that random dude on the street), you may have more trouble connecting to the magic you perform with that grimoire. Conversely, if the book holds the energy of a close family member or friend and it makes you happy every time you crack that spine, you will probably be able to perform lots of powerful magic with that book.

-Don't get discouraged if you try to cleanse the lingering energy of a hand-me-down grimoire and it doesn't work. The energy that clings to old books is strong, potent and stickier than gum on the bottom of your shoe. It's common for an old book to hold the energy of the previous owners, even after multiple cleansing spells.

-If you don't like the energy of your hand-me-down grimoire, consider jotting down on the spells in a brand new notebook. That way you can forge a connection between yourself and the old grimoire's spells, and use them without taking on the energy of the previous spell book. The act of rewriting a spell in your own book, with your own handwriting, is powerful.

-Notice when it's time for you to pass a grimoire on to the next witch. Just because a grimoire made its way across the universe to you doesn't mean you are the rightful owner of that grimoire *forever* (but maybe you are). Perhaps after a few weeks, years, or even decades, you sense that your hand-me-down grimoire is calling out for its next owner. More on that later in this book!

Homemade Grimoires

If you feel crafty and creative, you can make your own grimoire. They don't call it witch*craft* for nothing! Ha! Sorry—bad joke. I can't help myself sometimes.

I am a huge fan of making your own magical tools because it allows you to pour your inner power into a project. Then, when you use that magical tool, you'll be able to access that beautiful, creative energy that seeped into your grimoire during its creation. Cool, right? I've gotten wonderful results with my homemade magical tools because they are "supercharged" with my own personal energy.

Another benefit to making your own grimoire is that you will create a strong bond between you and your grimoire immediately. Your energy will mesh perfectly with your grimoire because it's the same exact energy.

Also, creating is manifesting—it's magic. When you make your own grimoire you are making something from nothing. You are taking something that was only the tiny seed of a thought in your mind and bringing it into the physical realm. You are using the thoughts of your mind (energy) to create change in your physical reality.

This potent manifesting energy will then find its way into any spell, intention or incantation that you jot down in your magical book.

Notebooks and Journals

If you want to keep this simple, start with a notebook or journal that you find at an office supply store, a local bookstore, or online.

Novelty Journals

I really enjoy those leather-bound unlined journals that have a metal latch to keep it closed. I've seen some with those gold-edged pages that are absolutely gorgeous. Usually, they are small enough to slide into a backpack or tote bag, and they can totally be disguised as a regular diary if you don't want your loved ones to know about your magical practice.

Before you purchase one of these novelty journals, think about your personal preferences. Do you prefer writing on a blank page or on neat little lines? Choose accordingly!

Are you going to want to tear out pages of this grimoire for specific spells (such as burning or burying pages)? In that case, look for a journal with perforated edges.

Be honest with yourself. Are you going to be OK with writing in your beautiful leather grimoire, or will you be tempted to keep it looking pristine? A grimoire is meant to be written in! You don't want to carry a fancy grimoire around only to constantly worry about ruining it. Your grimoire should feel special, but not precious.

Cheap Notebooks

Remember, your grimoire doesn't have to be fancy! Heck, you can even use a notebook you have lying around your house and turn it into a powerful, spell-packed grimoire. It doesn't even need to have a cover. A legal pad could work for some witches. If you go this route, my recommendation is to at least use a notebook that hasn't been written in yet. There's something really satisfying and exciting about opening up a fresh notebook full of smooth, blank sheets of paper.

I use cheap spiral notebooks all the time for grimoires, journals, and business planning. I like picking a color that makes me feel happy. Unlike with a fancy leather-bound diary, I have no qualms about scribbling down spells, drawing sigils and composing hilariously terrible poems. I'm not worried about writing "dumb" stuff in my notebook grimoire because I know I can buy another one next time I'm at the dollar store. The interesting thing is that I usually fill every page of these notebooks, but the nicer journals end up with lots of blank pages after a couple months of use. I think this has more to do with my personality than anything else.

Some witches love fancy notebooks because they feel inherently special and magical. Some witches opt for the cheap, 70-page spirals they used in school. Try one and see what you like! Or be like me and try both! Whatever!

Personalizing Your Notebook

If you want to jazz up your cheap notebook a bit, glue snapshots or images from magazines onto the cover. Wind colored ribbon or yarn through the metal spirals. Dab on puff paint or sprinkle glitter on the front. If you have old tarot or oracle decks, use your favorite cards to decorate your cover. Get as creative as you want, and go into this with a sense of playfulness and joy. Don't worry about being perfect, because last I checked, perfect doesn't exist. Let the cover of your notebook explode with your beautiful, wild magical energy.

Binders and Repurposed Books

If you want to get more involved in the creation of your grimoire, consider using a binder or a repurposed book!

Three-Ringed Binders

There are several advantages to using a binder as your grimoire. For starters, you can add or take out pages without leaving tears. You can reorganize your spells whenever you want, moving them around as you expand your magical practice.

If you get the binder with the clear plastic covering, you can create a vision board collage and switch it out every year or every season. I did this with one of my first grimoires. I bought a cheerful hot pink binder and glued quotes and pictures that represented all the things I wanted to manifest. That was in 2017 and almost all of those things have manifested now—many of them without me performing specific spells to create those results! I looked at my vision board every time I pulled out my grimoire, and I think that consistent repetition created some powerful momentum in the universe.

I personalized my binder in other ways, too. I enjoyed typing up my spells and making pretty printables of my incarnations and altar setups to keep in my three-ring grimoire. Color-coordinated tabs and markers helped me stay organized while making each page look bright and fun. (I'm really into colors when it comes to my art, home decor and witchy tools, but every witch is different! If you're not into colors, use black ink or #2 pencils only. All that matters is that the aesthetics of your grimoire resonate with you.)

You can further personalize your binder by *making* your sheets of paper. That's right—**homemade paper.** There are many great YouTube videos that walk you through how to do this. Full disclosure, it's not the quickest, easiest way, but how cool would it be to write your spells on paper that you made with love and care? I've seen some variations of this where witches add seeds into the paper pulp and then bury these pages in the earth after writing down their intentions. Once the paper is buried, the embedded seeds will grow. As the plant manifests, so will your desire.

Repurposed Books

To make a grimoire out of a repurposed book, find an old book with a lot of pages and a sturdy binding. This can be a book you love or just a book you were drawn to.

(Make sure your energy is compatible with the book's energy. Just like with hand-me-down grimoires, old books tend to hold the energy of all the previous owners. If you sense any sort of discomfort when you're holding the book, choose a different book to use or perform some cleansing spells on the book before you begin repurposing it.)

Once you've chosen your book, cut blank sheets of paper (plain or lined) and adhere the pieces of paper to both sides of each page. Now you have a vintage-looking blank book just waiting for you to scribble down all your witchy thoughts in!

This is a nice solution if you want to keep your witchcraft on the down-low. Everyone else will see you carrying around an old copy of Great Expectations, and your witchy leanings will be your little secret.

You can go one step further and wrap the cover in cloth or paper. If you're a stitch witch, you can crochet a book sleeve to wrap around the cover.

Going Totally DIY

For those brave, super-crafty witches out there, you can make the entire book yourself! Start by cutting out sheets of paper and attaching them to a cardboard (or card stock) cover.

This is ideal if you are particular about the size of your grimoire and the number of pages it contains. To add a bit of magic to your project, use meaningful numbers when you decide on the dimensions of your spell book. For example, you can make your book have 77 or 222 pages (aligned numbers), and you can design your cover to be five inches by five inches to draw from the power of a five-pointed pentagram.

The binding of your DIY book can be as simple as a few staples, or you can get more elaborate by sewing the binding with a needle and thread. There are some great bookbinding YouTube videos if you want some ideas for how to do this.

Other Fun Ways to Spruce Up Your Homemade Grimoire

-Use tea bags to dye your pages and give them that old, magical look.

-Burn the edges of your pages for a raw-edged effect. (If you try this, be sure to practice fire safety!)

-Use an old-fashioned fountain pen to elevate the energy of your grimoire.

Tips For Using A Homemade Grimoire

-Allow this to be a work in progress. Don't wait for your DIY grimoire to be completely done before you start using it. You'll add more personal touches and meaningful decorations each time you sit down with your grimoire. Let your grimoire grow and change along with you.

-Release any judgments that come up as you create! You are beautiful, powerful, and full of magic. Whatever happens when you're working on your grimoire is part of your magical journey. Embrace the messiness and celebrate your individuality! Don't compare your grimoire to anyone else's. Your magic comes from who YOU are.

-Be aware of your thoughts, feelings and energy when you're making your grimoire. The energy you experience when you are making your grimoire will flow into and remain within the pages, binding, and cover of your book for years to come. If you are working on your grimoire and you feel upset, angry, bitter, drained or any other unwanted emotion, set aside your project and do something else. Take a walk, call a friend, soak in a bathtub—do something that will shift your energy. Come back to your grimoire-making project when you're feeling better.

Digital Grimoires

Where my tech witches at? I wrote this just for you. If you're not into the whole "book thing", you can try this eco-friendly, super convenient grimoire alternative —a digital grimoire!

A digital grimoire is any collection of spells or magical writing that exists in some kind of electronic or web-based form. Yes, a digital grimoire is just as powerful as any other form of grimoire, and it brings along many other benefits.

You can take this kind of grimoire with you wherever you go. Whether you have it typed up on the notepad app on your phone or log into a personal blog with links to your favorite magical videos and tried-and-true spells.

If you want to see an example of a web-based grimoire, check out my website www.whitewitchacademy.com. I've spent lots of time posting printables, videos, articles and other magical resources for others to learn from. Plus, I've got a free ebook that also doubles as a grimoire! You can get that at www.whitewitchacademy.com/freebies.

Social Media Grimoire

Social media platforms change really quickly these days. By the time you're reading this, Tik Tok might be so five minutes ago. If I mention things that aren't cool anymore, substitute the social media platform of your choice. I want to give you some ideas so you can explore the possibilities on your own!

Pinterest is a photo-based platform that allows you to create "boards" with different themes and "pin" images to each of these boards. There are a TON of awesome witchy articles, infographics, and free printables floating around Pinterest for you to collect and arrange on your digital grimoire board. You can also follow other witches who are actively posting and pining their favorite pins.

Instagram is another photo-based platform where you can see how other witches are casting spells and setting up their altars. There's a feature where you can bookmark other people's posts, so you can go back and look at them later. You can also use your account to add photos of your own witchy lifestyle. With the option to keep your account private, you don't have to worry about other people seeing your posts if you don't want them to.

Facebook has hundreds of witch-themed groups you can join if you want to be part of an online community of like-minded people who talk about magic and their experiences with the craft. A simple search in the search bar will bring up all the relevant groups. Request to join a few and see which ones match your energy. I've been in groups that do live streams, hold free tarot readings, and answer member questions. This is a great option if you don't live near any witches and you want to connect with people who are on the same path as you! If you don't like a group, leave and find another one.

Tik Tok also has a thriving magical community where lots of witches (including yours truly) upload their own short and snappy magical videos. The videos are all sixty seconds or less, so you can browse the platform whenever you have a minute of free time.

> Note: Backup *all* of your social media content somewhere else such as an external hard drive or internet-based storage. That way, if your social media account gets suspended or closed for whatever reason, you won't lose your entire collection of spells!

Blog Grimoire

You can create your own witchy blog (and keep it private or share it with the world—your call). Another option is to use someone else's blog as your go-to grimoire. When I first started out, I had two or three blogs that I checked regularly for new spells and magical tips. Let me warn you—not everything you read on the Internet is true. I know. Total shocker, right?

But seriously—and actually this goes for ANYTHING, not just witchcraft—pass every nugget of info through the filter of your intuition. Explore the spells you feel drawn to, and set aside the rest. If something didn't work for you, that doesn't mean it won't work for someone else. On the flip side, a spell that you swear by might be a total dud for the next witch.

Google Docs, Word Processor, or Electronic Folder

Copy and paste website links, images, and bits of text into a Google Doc or whatever app or word processor you like to use. Add, edit, and move around sections as you gain more experience in your witchcraft and watch your digital grimoire grow. This is a simple, private, convenient way to save all your spells without a paper trail. The other nice thing about this format is you can easily share it with a friend via email or a private link! Some web-based word processors allow you to collaborate with others. That means all the witches in your coven can log into a document and add their magical notes in real time!

Ebooks and PDFs

I mentioned my free ebook grimoire you can download off my site at www.whitewitchacademy.com/freebies. There are lots of other ebook grimoires available online, and the ebook version of a published grimoire is usually a heck of a lot cheaper than the print copy. It's also a lot easier to carry around a phone, tablet, or ebook reader rather than a mammoth encyclopedia-style spell book. Kindle books now includes a notes feature where you can highlight and bookmark your most used spells.

Tips For Using A Digital Grimoire

-Start with your preferred tech platform for your first digital grimoire. When you're adding entries or reading through your grimoire, you want it to feel comfortable and easy. Using your grimoire shouldn't feel intimidating or like a chore. When in doubt, switch to a different tech platform, or try using a hard copy.

-You can try having a hybrid digital/paper grimoire by collecting spells in a digital document and printing it out periodically. It's the best of both worlds!

-Make sure you back your digital grimoire up somewhere! Have you ever been almost done with a paper for school or work only to have your computer crash. It's the worst. Don't let this happen to your grimoire.

-Label all your files with simple headings so you can easily find what you need when you need it!

-Be EXTRA careful about using your digital grimoire during Mercury Retrograde. I feel like my technology gets a bit glitchy every time this comes around.

Unconventional Grimoires

If you think your spell book actually has to be a book, think again! Grimoires, like witches, come in all shapes and sizes. There are absolutely, positively, no rules for what your grimoire needs to look like. It doesn't even have to contain words! Check out these unconventional, powerful grimoires you can create.

Box O Spells

I'm sure there are witches all over the place doing this, but I got the idea from Carrie Green, an intuition-based entrepreneur. I ordered a planner from her and it came in a beautiful box. There were instructions on this box that said something like, "This is more than a box, it's a tool for manifestation. Whatever is in this box, is."

I filled that box with things I wanted to manifest—fancy perfume, a list of goals, crystals, money, a description of the man I wanted to marry, and some handwritten incantations to add a little magic to my box. As the year went on, I wrote out more spells and placed them in the box. After a while, I realized I had turned my manifestation box into a full-fledged grimoire.

Any box can serve as a grimoire. Instead of writing in the pages of a book, you can gather up all your doodles, quotes, magical poems, and anything else you feel applies to your magical practice, and place all of it in a box.

If you want to get a little more organized, you can color code your pieces of paper or paperclip similar spells together.

Just like with a book, make sure the box feels "special". Get a beautiful wood-carved box, or take a shoebox and bedazzle it with your glitter and rhinestones!

Scrapbook/Collage Grimoire

When I was in middle school, scrapbooking was a popular activity. I'm not totally sure why a bunch of rowdy thirteen-year-olds were into this, but whatever.

Kids in my class would bring out their colorful cut-out borders and fancy scissors to create beautiful arrangements of photos. Each page would have a theme and a color scheme. Then they'd use calligraphy pens to jot down captions below each picture.

If you want to "scrapbook" your grimoire, take a trip to the local craft store and pick up some supplies—decorative paper, rainbow pens, ribbons, labels, and a binder with those plastic-covered sticky sheets. Consider meditating before you go to the store so you feel connected to your intuition as you shop.

Create each page of your grimoire just as you would a scrapbook. Split the book into sections and plan out a specific theme for each page such as Rose Quartz magic, love potion recipes, sabbat altars, and more! Find ways to convey your spells through photos, cut-outs, and symbols rather than a whole page of text. Get creative and have fun! This could make a thoughtful gift for a new witch if you ever decide to part with it.

Embroidered Quilt

If you are a skilled stitch witch, you can use a quilt as your grimoire. Embroider sigils, incantations, and correspondences on the squares. Use fabric from your old altar cloths and pick colors that are meaningful to you.

How exquisite would it feel to curl up in your

magical grimoire blanket in front of a crackling fire on a crisp autumn evening while meditating on your deepest desires? It almost makes me want to take up sewing—almost.

Deck of Magical Spell Cards

I created an oracle deck (and I'm going to bring it back really soon; I promise!) that taught witchcraft in a simple way. The guidebook had everything you needed to practice witchcraft, and each card featured a common magic tool. This deck became a sort of grimoire that I took with me when I was living a nomadic lifestyle. I didn't have room for magical tools or heavy books, so this deck was my way to condense my entire witchcraft practice into something that would fit in the pocket of a backpack. There are other decks out there that are witchcraft-focused and include a variety of useful spells. Check out the metaphysical section of your local bookstore for some options!

Sketch Pads and Coloring Books

An art witch casts spells through the act of making art! Consider creating a grimoire of spells using only sketches, images, and sigils. I have a friend who makes the most amazing grimoire coloring books. They're in a series called, "The

Coloring Book of Shadows". (You can find them at www.whitewitchacademy.com/resources). There are few words in her grimoires because most of the magic comes from coloring in the witchy imagery she created.

Wall Mural Grimoire

If you're a visual artist, you might enjoy creating and using a wall mural grimoire. Designate a wall in your home (or garage) and start painting. Paint whatever comes to mind and select colors intuitively. Write down your spells with markers, and paint over them when you run out of space. Let the wall transform as you deepen your magical practice.

I saw someone turn one of their office walls into a huge chalkboard. She uses it to plot out stories for her books and brainstorm business ideas. It's a grimoire of sorts—a way for her to tap into her power and magic by taking her thoughts out of her head and into a physical world where she can begin to act on them.

What To Put In Your Grimoire

I f you have your grimoire, and it's not already filled with spells, you might be wondering something along the lines of, "What in the world am I supposed to put in this grimoire?"

Guess what? You're in excellent company. The witches who came before you faced that same question.

For me, the answer is simple.

PUT WHATEVER YOU WANT.

Yes, I said it. Don't roll your eyes at me.

Here are my reasons:

1. Sometimes the most random thoughts are actually gems of wisdom that float up from your intuition. Whenever I actively stop judging and

overthinking everything, I surprise myself with how insightful I am.

2. Anything that goes into your magical grimoire is more likely to manifest. Because your grimoire is inherently powerful, that power can't help but trickle into the words and drawings filling those pages. Each time you add something to your grimoire, you channel that power.

3. You have absolute control of your grimoire. It is your energetic sandbox to play in whenever you want. You don't have to show it to anyone else if you don't want to. If you write something you no longer resonate with, cross it out. If you're concerned someone will sneak a peek at your magical notes, create a code and write your most personal spells using a language only you know! You are also totally welcome to tear out pages, burn them, bury them, scribble pink highlighter all over them. Don't filter yourself. For some witches, their grimoire is the only place they get to be who they are!

Here's a list of things you can put in your grimoire:

Remember, this list is only a starting point. I'm sure you've got some fantastic ideas of your own to add!

Spells

- Rewrite or print out common spells off the Internet (usually this is fine if it's for personal use).
- Write your own spells. (Check out the next chapter for my guide for spell-writing.)
- Leave a section after each spell to note the results of a particular spell.

Drawings

- Sketch out sigils to use for future spells
- Draw a picture of your altar so you can recreate it when you perform the spell again.
- Doodle out your ideas for sabbat and esbat decorations. (Sabbats are witch holidays and esbats are lunar-theme ceremonies.)

Magical Objects

- Press flowers, herbs, leaves, and feathers between the pages.

- Hide bits of ribbon, thread, locks of hair, or yarn that you've used for spells in your book
- Use your favorite tarot cards to bookmark notable spells.

Coven Info

- Dedicate a section of your grimoire to note the names and contact info of the members of your coven.
- Make notes each time you meet up, such as what spells you perform, what you talk about, and what is happening in the lives of your fellow witches.
- If you don't have a coven, journal about your ideal group of magical friends, and doing that will energetically invite these people into your life.

Visualization Entries

- Write out a scene from your ideal life (or your life after your spell has manifested). Include sensory details, the feel of your clothing, the scents in the air and everything you see and experience in this

THE BEGINNER WITCH'S GUIDE TO GRIMIORES

vision. Pretend you are the future you and you're writing a journal entry for a typical day. If you do this consistently, you'll likely see the universe presenting you with exciting opportunities.

Recipes

- Jot down your favorite kitchen magic recipes.
- Plan weekly grocery lists.
- List out all the herbs you are growing in your garden and what kind of magic you plan on using them for.
- Create your own herbal, fruit, and vegetable correspondences. For example, you may decide that you associate cherries with relaxation because you eat them in the summer when you have more free time.

Imagery

- Photos, inspirational cutouts from magazines, paintings, and any other visual imagery can add color and beauty to your grimoire.

Poems

- Compose couplets, traditional incantations, limericks, haikus, nursery rhyme, song lyrics, or free form poetry.

Journal Entries

- Write about the highs and lows of your day.
- Get as detailed as you want! You're never going to bore your grimoire.

Correspondences

- Make a list of all the colors, crystals, numbers, and tarot cards you use in your magic and write a few words you associate with each one. For me, I associate yellow with success, happiness, and ambition. The color red makes me think of power, courage, and determination. You might have different associations based on your culture and environment.

Life Goals

- When I was starting my witchy business, I wrote all about my ideas, business expenses, and financial goals in my grimoire.
- Journal about your relationships with your loved ones, or set intentions to cultivate other relationships.
- Jot down everything you eat if you are working on improving your diet. Note the lunar cycle or any astrological events to see if any patterns show up.

How To Write Your Own Grimoire Spells

If you are staring at a blank grimoire and you want to try your hand at writing your own spells, **here's a simple method I use to create powerful, personalized spells that work!**

Basically, incantations work because words are powerful. When you take a thought or desire and turn it into a statement, you are manifesting. This is the same concept behind affirmations. If you want to shift your current reality, stay by speaking your intention aloud (or in your head).

"I am powerful."

"I am beautiful."

"I am an internationally-known writer."

"My screenplay sells for $100,000."

"My house is steps away from the ocean and I fall asleep listening to the waves each night."

As someone who has studied and experimented with the Law of Attraction, personal development, and witchcraft, I've found that my spells manifest best if I write or spell my intention in this format.

Here Are My Tips

1. Your intention should be written or spoken in the first person (if the spell is to manifest something for yourself).

The reason for this is that I want to be as clear as possible that this is my spell and I, the spell-caster, am the one who is sending out this desire so that it may manifest in my life.

2. Your intention should be written or spoken in the present tense.

This is important because if you say "I will sell my screenplay for $100,000", then your spell holds the energy of you receiving this desire in the future. When you say, "I will", that implies you don't currently have your desire. Though I do think it's important to acknowledge the present situation (though not all witches agree with me), I believe that when you are actively casting a spell, you should shift your energy AS MUCH AS POSSIBLE to the energy you will feel and experience once the desire has manifested. To do this, it helps to speak the intention as if it has currently manifested.

3. The focus on your intention needs to be on the positive, not the negative.

Think about what you'll gain from your spell, not what you'll lose.

Example: "I walk along the beach in a bikini and I smile as I savor the experience of feeling beautiful in my body." This is an intention where the focus is on attracting positive attention, feeling good in your skin, and enjoying your time at the beach.

"I lose twenty-five pounds so I can look good in my bikini." This statement, although it follows the other guidelines, is focusing on losing weight— LOSING being the key word. Lose, decrease, zero, no are all negative-focused words that can add unnecessary resistance to your spells. I'm not saying don't use them in conversation, but I am saying that these kinds of words might cause your spells to manifest slower (or not at all).

Another example I hear a lot is witches casting spells with the intention, "I am debt-free". The focus is on debt—a negative focus. Instead try something like, "I have more than enough money to cover all of my bills and my savings account grows every day."

Note: You might be wondering why these intentions aren't written in rhymes like traditional spells —sometimes called incantations. The reason I teach this is because I find that having my intention be close to the way I normally speak makes me feel a stronger connection to it.

Historically, spells were shared from witch to witch through short, easy-to-remember rhymes, poems, or songs. Because witchcraft was highly controversial in those times (sometimes even considered a crime), witches chose not to write their spells down to keep from getting caught practicing magic.

If you want to write a spell that rhymes, go for it. See if it makes you feel witchy and powerful. If I ever cast a spell with a rhyme, I will still follow those three guidelines.

I always encourage witches to try writing their own spells—even if they're just starting out! I almost always create my own intentions and incantations, rather than using spells out of books. I think that the words I put together come from a deep magical place inside of me—my inner wisdom. I think we are all born with powers and ancient knowledge, and writing spells is a way to directly tap into that part of ourselves. If you've never tried writing your own spells, give it a try and see what kind of results you get!

How To Shift The Energy

If you suspect your intention isn't as powerful as I could be, take a moment to examine it using the three guidelines I've shared here, and see if you can revise it. Then speak the intention aloud and see how it makes you feel. Do you feel excited? Happy? Optimistic? That's when you know you've got a winner.

Caring For Your Grimoire

A grimoire, like most magical tools, takes some time to get used to and form a bond with. Don't rush this. It's a relationship, and relationships happen gradually. When you are first using your grimoire, give yourself at least a month to get comfortable with it.

It's like when you buy a new yearly planner. In the early months, the planner might feel unfamiliar and awkward, but by the end of the year, your planner—now a bit tattered and filled with notes and doodles—feels as familiar as an old friend.

During the first month with your new grimoire, spend as much time with it as you can. Sleep with it near your bed, tuck it away in your tote bag, and leaf through it while you're waiting for the barista to finish making your latte. Bring it with you on walks and take notes in the margins as you sit in the shade of your favorite tree. Talk to it, sing it a lullaby, and tell it your deepest, darkest secrets. Your grimoire will always be loyal to you. Don't be afraid to let it get banged up, spilled on, or torn. None of that will lessen the magical energy it holds. Just like a well-worn stuffed animal, grimoires are meant to be loved!

If you still have trouble connecting with your grimoire, try performing a cleansing spell on it. This is especially important if the book has been exposed to lots of different energies.

For example, a hand-me-down book will hold the energy of the previous owner. In some cases, this is a good thing, but at other times, the energy is incompatible with your personal energy.

Published books you pick up at a bookstore or order online may also hold some funky energy. Think of all those people who have interacted with the book before it got to you—people involved in the book's printing, the people who shipped the book, the people who shelved the book, and anyone who happened to pick up and page through the book while browsing the store. That's a whole hodgepodge of energy!

Cleansing may help you create an energetic "blank slate". It will wipe away any unwanted energy and prepare it for your own unique energetic thumbprint.

You might notice that your grimoire's energy

feels different from day to day. Just like a person, the energy of an object can fluctuate. To counter this, take a moment to sense the grimoire's energy each time you use it. Hold it in your arms and notice the thoughts, feelings, and images that flit through your mind. These thoughts could be a reaction to the current energy of your grimoire. If you find yourself having unwanted thoughts or emotions when you are holding your grimoire, perform a cleansing spell on the book. This is especially important if you recently used the grimoire in a very intense spell.

Here Are My Favorite Methods of Cleansing:

Sacred Space Cleansing

Find a space in your home or outside where you feel relaxed. If possible, try to keep people from coming into your space or interrupting you. Arrange magical tools and trinkets around you to create an atmosphere for magic. This can include candles, incense, crystals, essential oil diffusers, or anything else that "elevates" the space.

You can also create a meditation playlist with your favorite calming songs. And don't forget to brew a cup of tea or other relaxing beverage if that's something you enjoy.

Once the energy feels desirable, spend some

time in that space while you interact with your grimoire. Write down spells, scribble journal entries, or read through your grimoire. Just having your grimoire in this calm, high-vibrational space will help cleanse it. The surrounding energy of the room will sink into the pages of the grimoire and make that book more aligned to who you are.

Cleansing White Light Meditation

Perform a white light meditation while hugging the grimoire to your chest. To do this, start by closing your eyes and listening to your breath. Notice your inhales and exhales, notice the stability of the earth underneath you.

When you feel grounded, visualize a white light moving down from the sky. This is the cleansing white light of the universe. Invite it to wash over you and float into your grimoire. Then let overflow from the pages and allow it to fill the entire space. As it fills the room, it will gently guide any negative or unwanted energy away from you and your grimoire.

I recommend doing this meditation for about five to ten minutes, but feel free to go longer or shorter as you feel guided. When you feel like you've done the job, open your eyes.

Crystal Cleansing

Selenite and smoky quartz are my favorite crystals for energetically cleansing spells. All you have to do is place the crystal on top of or inside your grimoire and leave it there for ten minutes or so. When you come back to your grimoire, practice "sensing the energy" of the book. Does it feel any different? The changes can be subtle or dramatic.

If the answer is no, leave the crystal with your grimoire for another five minutes. You can also use this method with certain "cleansing" tarot cards such as Temperance, the Moon, and the Star.

When To Release A Well-Loved Grimoire

It doesn't matter what kind of grimoire you have—published, hand-me-down, electronic, or something less traditional—sometimes a grimoire will ask to be passed on to another witch. This can happen with any magical tool, not just grimoires. It's a natural process. A powerful witch knows that there are beginnings and there are ends. **Here are some signs that your grimoire is ready to connect with someone new:**

A new grimoire comes into your life and you find yourself no longer drawn to your previous grimoire.

Often, when you invite something new into your life, you naturally begin to let go of something that is no longer serving you. Think about the leaves that fall off trees in the winter and grow back every spring. Nature is a perfect example of letting go of the past in the right way, at the right time.

If you acquire a new grimoire (by purchasing it, making it, or receiving it as a gift) and you find yourself using it almost exclusively, this could be a sign that it's time to pass along your old grimoire. Give yourself a little time to make sure you feel well connected to your new grimoire. Don't force yourself to keep using the old grimoire. Value yourself enough to let go of whatever isn't serving you anymore, so that you can allow yourself to grow and flow with the universe.

Keep your eyes open for people or organizations you can give your old grimoire to and allow yourself to be guided by the universe. If you don't know what to do with your old grimoire, let it sit on your shelf for a while before you do anything.

You keep losing or misplacing your grimoire.

If you misplace your grimoire one or two times, I wouldn't make any assumptions based on that. However, if you see a pattern where you are continually leaving your grimoire in random places or losing it around your home, you might be ready for a new grimoire.

THE BEGINNER WITCH'S GUIDE TO GRIMIORES

A close friend mentions they are looking for a new grimoire.

If a loved one begins practicing witchcraft or they are on the lookout for a new grimoire, notice the thoughts and feelings that come up for you when they talk about this in front of you. Do you feel an intuitive nudge to gift them your grimoire? Does it make you feel excited and joyful when you think about giving them your grimoire?

If so, consider letting your friend borrow your grimoire to use for a day or two, or invite them to perform magic with you while you both use the grimoire. You can also copy down a few spells or tear out a page to give to your friend.

If you feel resentful, uncomfortable, or unsure that they will treat your grimoire with respect, this person might not be the right person for your grimoire.

It's also helpful to ask that person how *they* feel about working with your grimoire. See if they are experiencing any intuitive nudges to invite this grimoire into their magical practice. Don't push them. Let them know that it's a deeply personal choice, and it's totally fine if they don't feel a connection to your grimoire. Maybe your grimoire is meant to be given to someone else.

Finally, you make sure you are truly ready to let go, otherwise you might worry about how your friend is caring for your grimoire. Remember the man who gave me his grimoire on the street? I threw out his grimoire almost immediately after he handed it to me. I doubt he knew or ever looked back. I never saw him again. He seemed to be ready to give that grimoire away to me with no strings attached. That's how you want to feel before you actually decide to pass on your magical book.

You notice the spells you perform with your grimoire aren't as effective.

OK, to be fair, there could be many reasons why your spell didn't work that have absolutely nothing to do with your grimoire. If you want to learn more about that, check out my book *Why Didn't My Spell Work?*.

If you are seeing a pattern where the spells you perform with your grimoire aren't manifesting, I would suggest you perform your cleansing method of choice (maybe more than once) and see if that changes things.

If not, ask the universe to send you a grimoire that is well suited to who you are and what kind of magic you are drawn to. Check out your favorite bookstores, read over your go-to witchy blogs, and ask around to see if anyone has any leads on a good grimoire. Then let the universe work. See what crosses your path. Perhaps all you need is a new grimoire to open up your natural flow of magic.

What if you made a mistake and you want your grimoire back?

I'm going to tell you the same thing I tell myself whenever I go down the winding path of regret. There are no mistakes, my witchy friend. None.

I have a hard time breaking up with men who aren't totally right for me. I'll know in my heart that the relationship isn't working, and I'll actually sit down and have the "breakup conversation". But then I'll eventually get back together with them. I'll tell myself that I was overreacting, that I was self-sabotaging, that I need to stop being so picky, etc.

Inevitably, the relationship will fall apart again—every single time.

I believe there's a special sort of power that happens when you make a decision. Even if you make your choice and feel awful about it afterward, there was SOME reason you made that choice in the first place, and it was probably a good reason.

If you give your grimoire away and you regret it, you can always ask for it back. Sometimes, the person says yes, or sometimes the universe will bring that grimoire back to you in a totally organic way.

Regardless, *you* made the decision in the first

place, and I personally believe that whatever happens after that decision is something you were meant to experience—good or bad.

So be brave and bold, my witchy friend. You can't choose wrong.

I can't tell you how many times I've given something up without knowing what was right around the corner. The universe is full of wonderful surprises. Make space for them.

Final Thoughts

You And Your Grimoire

Let your grimoire be a reflection of who you currently are! I know I've said this a lot, but I'll say it again: Don't be afraid to mess up your grimoire. Seriously. Your grimoire shouldn't feel stuffy or pretentious. **In fact, I hope NOTHING in your witchcraft practice feels stuffy or pretentious!**

It's totally fine if your grimoire smells like a campfire, has pages stuck together with wax, and if some words aren't legible. The more time you spend with your grimoire, the more it will reflect who you are. *You* have scars, imperfections, crooked teeth, stretch marks, bad moods, moments of brilliance, and lots of free flowing creativity. **Your grimoire is going to be as perfectly imperfect as you are.**

My Thoughts On Using Multiple Grimoires

I believe a witch can use as many grimoires as they want throughout their lifetime. Many witches have multiple grimoires. I have at least five or six published grimoires that I look through when I need some ideas for spells. Some of these grimoires are general and cover a variety of topics. Others are specific to one area of magic, such as astrology, tarot, or potions.

I also have three spiral notebooks that serve as grimoires. One of them is more business-focused. Another is where I track my moods and physical changes while observing the different lunar cycles. I use the third notebook for stream of consciousness writing. I believe that scribbling down my random thoughts helps me stay in touch with my intuition, the guiding force behind my magic. When I read back over those entries, I often uncover limiting beliefs and blocks that have been creating resistance to my spells. Sometimes, I'll spot patterns such as specific worries that keep coming up. This is a great shadow work hack.

When it comes to more unconventional grimoires, I have a magical blog (which I mentioned), an oracle deck full of built-in spells, and a box of magical notes.

I tell you all that because **I want you to feel empowered to use a grimoire that meets you**

where you are. A grimoire is a powerful tool to deepen your witchcraft—the key word here is "YOUR". Not *my* witchcraft, not your *friend's* witchcraft, not your favorite witchy *celebrity's* witchcraft—YOUR witchcraft.

So what are you waiting for?

Crack open your grimoire and go cast a spell, you powerful, magical witch!

A Note From The Author

Hi there, Witch!

Thanks for picking up this book! I hope it helped you on your magical journey.

If you want to learn more ways to practice simple, secular witchcraft, be sure to pick up a copy of this book of spells, and my free Beginner Witch Starter kit with printables, correspondences, meditations, and magical journaling prompts. Use the link below to get both of those!

https://whitewitchacademy.com/freebies

Also, be sure to check out the other witchy books in the **White Witch Academy Textbook series.** You can find them here:

https://whitewitchacademy.com/books

If you're on social media,
follow me on Instagram or Tik Tok
@whitewitchacademy
Or send me an email at
julie@magicalpowerwithin.com

Lastly, **if you enjoyed this book leave a review so other witches can decide if this book is for them!** Reviews help me out so much and I appreciate the feedback.

Thank you for reading. I hope this book bought a little joy and magic to your life!

Until next time,

Julie Wilder

Also by Julie Wilder

What Type of Witch Are You?
How to Become A Witch
Why Didn't My Spell Work?
Beginner Witch's Guide to Grimoires
Tarot for Beginner Witches

☆